By Kerri Lane

Illustrated by Sarah Dunk

To my newest S.I.L., Michael M. –
This one is finally yours.
Love, K.

Pearson Australia
(a division of Pearson Australia Group Pty Ltd)
707 Collins Street, Melbourne, Victoria 3008
PO Box 23360, Melbourne, Victoria 8012
www.pearson.com.au

First published 2010 by Pearson Australia
2019 2018 2017 2016
10 9 8 7 6 5 4 3 2

Publisher: Simone Calderwood
Illustrator: Sarah Dunk
Editor: Fiona Cooke
Designer: Jennifer Johnston
Copyright & Picture Editor: Michelle Jellett
Project Editor: Aisling Coughlan
Production Controller: Claire Henry
Printed in Australia by the SOS Print + Media Group
ISBN 978 1 4425 2726 3

Pearson Australia Group Pty Ltd ABN 40 004 245 943

Contents

Chapter 1 Save Me! Somebody… Anybody… Please!! 5
Chapter 2 Snorkelling, Anyone? 12
Chapter 3 Hot Dog Versus Sweetie-Pie 19
Chapter 4 Need M8 27
Chapter 5 It's True, I'm Brilliant 32
Chapter 6 Bozo-Cam 34
Chapter 7 Dogs Are Disgusting! 40
Chapter 8 Good Doggie! 45
Chapter 9 Payback Time 51
Chapter 10 Go, Hot Dog! 55

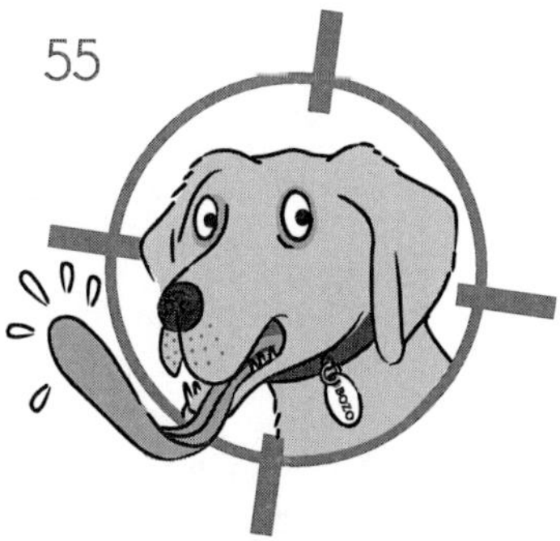

Chapter 1

Save Me! Somebody... Anybody... Please!!

I SQUINTED and took aim. Three more balloons to pop on the screen and I would have chalked up a record score. I lined them up.

Pop! Pop! Pop!

Take that! I was the champion! My name would go into the Balloon-Popping Hall of Fame.

I went to high-five my companion, but all I got back was a loud, gurgling snore. Hot Dog, the Fattest Sausage Dog in the World, lazily swatted a fly in his sleep and ignored me.

Great. This was what my life had become. Snoring dogs and boring computer games. Mum had confiscated all the good games. She was a cruel woman. I'm not kidding! She could teach torture tactics to government spies!

Hot Dog snored again.

I sighed and looked around my room for something to do. I couldn't believe it. Summer holidays and I was grounded. All because of one little remote-controlled helicopter that just happened to make contact with one little vase in the living room.

Mum didn't even like the vase! She reckoned that wasn't the point. She said a rule is a rule, and her rule was "No flying the helicopter in the house."

And so here I was, stuck at home with a seventeen-year-old sister who is seriously crazy and a sixteen-year-old brother who *could* be cool—if he'd ever learn to share. He's super-smart. He's an electronics geek, and he's got the coolest stuff.

Trouble is, I'm not allowed anywhere near it. Seriously.

I snuck into his room once and he found out. The next day, this plastic bag arrived on my desk. It had three fingers in it. Chopped-off fingers. Fingers severed from a hand…

Okay—so they were plastic, and the dripping blood was fake, but I got the message. I didn't even have to read the note (even though I did). It had four words:

Of course, I did what every little brother would do in that situation.

I dobbed on him.

Of course, *that* backfired because I'd forgotten that I'd already been warned to stay away from Sam's stuff. I copped a weekend grounding. *Another* one.

Talk about walking into your own trap…

That little episode left me with only one choice. Plan B: Find a way to sneak into Sam's room and not leave a trace!

It had been a cinch. He hadn't seen me, and he hadn't noticed anything was missing—and the camcorder was so tiny, I felt sure he wouldn't notice it was missing right away.

If he'd just leave his room again for a little while, it could be the one thing that might save me from this boring holiday.

It was just a pity I couldn't be saved from my sister. Angie chose that moment to storm into my room. Even Hot Dog jumped!

I sighed. "Can you read? Can't you see the sign?" I read it out for her.

Angie rolled her eyes. "Maybe you should remember that when you sneak into Sam's room when you think no-one is looking."

"Do not!"

"Do," she answered sweetly, pointing to the camcorder in my hand.

I was doomed. If Sam found out I'd been in there again, I could kiss my precious little pinkies goodbye. And all their buddies! But worse, if my folks found out, I could kiss all my holidays goodbye for the rest of my life!

This was bad. My heart seriously fell right out of my body and onto the floor in a big, gooey puddle. Because in my twelve years, I'd got to know my sister pretty well, and I knew what was coming.

Blackmail.

"W—what do you want?" I stammered.

Angie smiled. It was a cruel, evil smile. I knew it well.

"Your face," she answered.

Trapped in my own house. Trapped by my own stupidity.

"My face?" I repeated.

"Yes! I've got to trial this face mask for a survey company and you've got the perfect face for it!" she answered brightly.

A face mask! Not that! What would be next? Lipstick? Nail polish?

"Wait! My face is anything but perfect!" I said. "See? Zits! Blackheads! Whiteheads. I think I even saw some orangeheads in there! They're bad! Contagious! You don't want to go anywhere near this face!" I warned, backing away from her.

She kept coming at me. She was still smiling. "Don't be silly. It's the perfect face for this experiment. I only have one requirement: a face that's here, now." I'm sure she cackled then—and it was a scary sound. "And that's *your* face, little brother. Stand still!"

I was lost… and there was no-one to save me.

Hot Dog covered his eyes with his paws.

As Angie slathered sticky, rose-perfumed gunk on my face, I had one thought—if anyone happened to be watching through my bedroom window with a telescope, I'd have to leave town. The state. The country!

But then I remembered the camcorder, and a very sneaky thought popped into my brain. It came from nowhere.

I felt a smile start to break out. Maybe I could have some fun this holiday after all. It's true. I'm brilliant...

Chapter 2

Snorkelling, Anyone?

OKAY, SO MY PLAN did need some tweaking. Like, I had to wait till both Angie and Sam were out of the house. At the same time. And that was tough.

It was like they had this plan that one of them would be on watch all the time.

Which was exactly what Mum had probably told them to do …

But anyway, I figured I'd only need about fifteen minutes.

Luckily, the moment came sooner than I'd expected. It was about time something went my way!

Ange said this stuff had to be left on for an hour, so there I was, trapped in my room, staring out at the blue summer sky, wishing I was at the beach. Or anywhere else in the world.

I heard her call out that she was going to the shops for an hour. Then I heard Sam ask what I was doing.

Ange laughed when she replied. "Don't worry, with the stuff he's wearing, he won't be moving an inch!"

Angie is so funny… NOT.

That was one down. Now for Sam.

Then I had it! Sam had been told to watch the washing in case it rained…

A chuckle rumbled up from deep inside me.

I snuck along the hall and started creeping down the stairs. I was feeling pretty good, till I caught a glimpse of myself in the mirror. And nearly had a heart attack!

Oh no! The pink gunk! For one moment I'd forgotten. Heart racing, I streaked back to my room.

Problem—I had to get outside. But if I went outside with this stuff all over me, I'd risk the kind of humiliation a boy never recovers from. And if I removed it, then Angie would dob on me to Mum.

I let the problem roll over in my mind. Then I had it.

It took about a minute for me to find my snorkelling mask. Dragging it on, I could still see some pink, but unless you were close, it looked like zinc cream.

Finally, I made it outside.

Sam's bedroom faced the backyard and I hugged the wall as I slunk down the side.

Around the back, I was into open territory.

I got down on my belly and slithered along the grass, dragging the hose and sprinkler behind me.

It would have been easier if I'd been able to see! The heat was melting the pink gunk, and it was running into my eyes. *And* my mask was fogging up.

I was nearly in place when I froze.

Sam's voice!

My heart was pounding so hard it took a minute to work out he was on his phone.

I let out a deep breath.

Whew…

Now to put the rest of my plan into action.

The sprinkler was Dad's pride and joy. Its arms waved water around like a fountain. You could even direct it in two places at once. And that's what I did. One arm faced the nearly dry washing, the other faced Sam's window.

Oh, gee, the washing's going to get wet…

All I had to do was wait for Sam to take the bait. I swiped the inside of my mask to clear my vision. It only took about three seconds more before I heard him yell and take off out of his room. That just gave me time to pull the sprinkler out of sight and slip back in through the front.

There was no time to lose!

I darted straight through to the back of the house and locked the doors. That was to buy myself some time. Then I raced back upstairs and into Sam's room.

I moved like my pants were on fire and I scoped the place with the same speed. Just as I'd found the rest of the recording equipment that I wanted, I heard him pounding on the back door. "Matt! Open up!"

I tossed the equipment into my room and wandered down to let him in.

"Wha—?" I answered with a stretch and a yawn. "What's going on? You woke me up!"

Sam frowned at me from behind the pile of washing. "You're a freak. Who sleeps with a snorkelling mask on?"

The mask! I'd forgotten about it. Until then I'd been secretly thinking I was pretty smart. Still, it was only one little bitty mistake in an otherwise brilliant plan. And it had worked. I had all the equipment in my room to prove it.

Now I just had to set it all up and wait for the fun to begin…

Chapter 3

Hot Dog Versus Sweetie-Pie

"**DOGGIE-CAM!** You've got a tiny camcorder attached to Hot Dog! That's brilliant, Matt!"

My mate Jye flopped onto my bed and we both stared at the computer screen.

"So, what did you do?" he asked.

I grinned. "Sam was working on some hidden camera stuff last year. He doesn't use it now, so I just 'borrowed' it for a while. It hooks back to the computer so I can watch from here."

"So, what kind of stuff have you uncovered?" Jye asked.

My smile faded. "That's the thing—I haven't found anything. The plan was to catch Sam and Ange doing stuff I could hold over them for a change." I sighed. "But it would probably work better if Hot Dog actually had a life," I continued miserably. "All he does is eat and sleep!"

It was true. We watched for the next hour and the most energetic thing Hot Dog did was scratch himself. And even that was half-hearted, like he couldn't really be bothered.

"Why don't you try the cat?" suggested Jye.

"Sweetie-Pie? Use Sweetie-Pie? That cat is psycho!" I answered.

Jye nodded. "Exactly! And you'd get some great pictures. They might even get you out of house arrest."

It wasn't a bad plan, actually. I hadn't thought of Sweetie-Pie because I tried to never think of Sweetie-Pie. She was Dad's cat and she was always nice to him. To me, she was pure evil. And I had the scars to prove it.

Still, it was worth a try. Anything was better than the boredom of my life at the moment.

It took us a while, and a huge chunk of Polish sausage, to coax Sweetie-Pie to come to us—and all Jye's strength to hold her down while I attached the camera.

Then the doorbell rang and she took off! Thankfully we'd got the camera in place. She was so fast! Downstairs and straight to the door.

Wow! She was sure one little sticky beak!

We sat glued to the screen. It was like watching a movie!

Trouble was, we could only see at Sweetie-Pie's level. We saw Angie's feet walk to the door. Her squeal told us that the delivery man had just delivered MORE goodies for her to sample for the survey company.

This was a very black day for me. More samples! And unless I could get some really bad stuff on her, I was doomed.

We saw big feet wearing heavy boots clomp into the hallway. The delivery man was carrying in the box. He asked Angie to sign the docket but then told her he didn't have a pen, so she skipped off to get one.

Boring.

Jye pointed to the screen.

"Hey! My folks are doing that, too. Some of the products we've had to test are pretty cool!"

I rubbed my hands over the silky-smooth skin on my face as pink gunk-filled nightmares flooded back. "Not all of them," I muttered.

The man left and it was on again.

The one thing I wasn't ready for was the camera movement. Sweetie-Pie moved so fast that it was like being on a roller-coaster! I was still getting my tummy settled when she took off again.

Then it was warp speed towards the kitchen. And if I ever needed proof that she was one tough kitty, I had it right there. As she got near snoring Hot Dog, she skidded to a stop, and went over and batted him fair on the nose.

Poor Hot Dog!

"Get her, boy! Give her a bop right back!" I yelled at the screen. But he didn't. Hot Dog opened one eye, whined and then shuffled backwards out of her way.

"That cat is half tiger!" laughed Jye.

I wasn't laughing. Sweetie-Pie was about as sweet as lemon juice!

I didn't get much time to worry, though, because then she darted into the kitchen. And looked up.

Bingo!

There was Sam at the open fridge. And he was drinking milk straight out of the carton!

"*Yes!* Gotcha!" I cheered.

Mum hated it when we drank from the carton—and now I had the goods! He was going to be in such trouble—unless, of course, he decided to be nicer to me. Much nicer.

But then it got even better. Or maybe even worse…

Sam leaned down to Sweetie-Pie. "Here you go, kitty-cat. Have some milk."

Yes, that's right! He held the carton out so Sweetie-Pie could have a lick!

Eeewww!

MILK

Sweetie's tongue was swiping like a windscreen wiper on full speed.

Then Sam's voice drifted in again. "Don't drink it all. Better leave some for Matty."

"What? For Matty!" I started to get really mad then. I thought of all those times Sam had brought me a glass of milk—without me even asking.

The rat! He'd been cat-poisoning me!

I wondered whether I should declare war. But then I figured it was smarter to just wait until I could use this to my advantage. And boy, was he going to pay…

Chapter 4

Need M8

JYE DECIDED it was time to leave. I think he was scared I was going to offer him some milk!

Okay, so I was still pretty mad with Sam, but secretly I was just mad because he thought of the milk thing first. But mostly I was just excited because I finally had "the goods" on him. Something BIG.

Mum and Dad would NOT be happy.

Now I just had to get something on Angie. I rubbed my hands together—this was going to be so good …

I snuck down and left a little trail of sausage for Sweetie-Pie that led right to Angie's door. Of course, Sweetie-Pie took the bait and walked straight into Angie's room. She jumped up on the bed and I could see Angie lying there with her phone pressed to her ear.

A telephone conversation?

My heart sank. *Boring …*

Then I really listened. Not just any conversation. This was a boyfriend conversation.

Sweetie-Pie hopped onto Angie's tummy, and that put the camera right in her face.

Then it happened. There was Angie, making kissy noises right into the phone. And talking all that gooey love talk!

Priceless!

This was golden!

Oh, life was going to be so sweet from now on!

I was about to text Jye with the news when my phone vibrated in my hands. The message icon flashed and I pressed the display button. Then frowned as I read on.

> In trouble.
> Need M8. J

"In trouble. Need a mate. Jye," I muttered.

The "need a mate" thing was our code for "come over fast". Trouble was, I was grounded. Geez—Jye really must be worried if he'd forgotten that.

So I dialled his numbcr. It was timc to talk face-to-face. Or at least, voice-to-voice.

"What gives?" I asked as soon as he answered.

Jye sounded frightened. "Lots of the houses around here have had stuff stolen and the police have been here asking questions!"

"So? What's that got to do with you?"

He sighed. "Matt. All the places have one thing in common. Me. I've been mowing everyone's lawns for pocket money."

"Oh." It was all I could think to say. Suddenly, trying to catch Angie and Sam didn't seem that important.

"What are you going to do?" I finally asked.

"I don't know," he answered.

His voice sounded like it used to when we were little kids and Sam would chase us wearing a scary mask. After we hung up, I couldn't stop thinking about it.

I knew what it was like to have people blame you for things you hadn't done. Somehow, I always got the blame for everything. Okay— so maybe most things really were my fault, but it really stung when I got blamed for things that weren't.

I'd hate it if people thought I was a thief. And Jye would too, especially when he was innocent. I'd known him since we were little kids, and Jye wasn't a thief.

There was that time a year ago. The pies. The lady had given us an extra one by mistake. I'd already taken a huge bite before we realised.

We'd looked at each other and counted back—and yep—we'd had two each. It was a spare one! I was cheering, but not Jye. He made us take it back, bite missing and all.

I wasn't all that happy, till the lady gave us each a vanilla slice for being honest.

No, Jye wasn't a thief. I just had to find a way to prove that…

Chapter 5 It's True, I'm Brilliant

ABOUT THEN, I heard Mum arriving home and I bounded down the stairs. "Mum! Jye's in big trouble! I have to help him get out of it!"

Mum dumped the grocery bags and barely even looked at me. "It's not going to work, Matt. I'm standing firm. You're not talking your way out of being grounded this time."

"Please, Mum? I'm not kidding. You can ask his parents!" I gave her my most innocent look.

Maybe that's where everything went wrong, because she still wouldn't budge.

I sighed, trudged back up to my room and flopped back on the bed. The computer was still on cat-cam, but I barely noticed it.

The problems were:

1. Jye needed help
2. I was grounded and couldn't help.

We needed to get this sorted before Jye got thrown in the lock-up and had to eat brussels sprouts every day for the rest of his life!

My eyes flicked to the screen. And it hit me. It really was true. I am brilliant.

Chapter 6

Bozo-Cam

I COULDN'T take a chance on texting Jye in case he didn't get the message straight away. So, I rang him.

"I can't get out, but I've had this awesome idea. But first of all, tell me what's been stolen. Is it big stuff?"

"No. Little things. Watches, jewellery, cash, electronic games and trinkets."

I frowned into the phone. "What are trinkets?"

"I'm not really sure. Mum said they're like ornaments and things."

"Wow!" I thought of all the ornaments here they could have. I'd even help pack them up. Mum has some really ugly stuff hanging around this place.

There was silence for a minute and then Jye said, "So, what is this awesome idea?"

"Doggie-cam!" I said the words in this really dramatic way and waited for him to tell me I was brilliant.

He didn't.

Instead he said, "How would that work? You haven't even had anything stolen."

"No, we use the doggie-cam to scope the neighbourhood! We need to see who's sneaking into the houses!"

Jye was obviously too upset to think clearly. "But Hot Dog doesn't move and Sweetie-Pie is a crazy cat! She'd never stay still!"

I sighed. "Listen, you're not looking at the big picture. It's a perfect plan. All we need is a well-behaved dog that will do as it's told. Any clues, yet?"

"Pardon?" Jye answered.

I sighed again. Louder. "YOUR dog. Bozo! Unlike some dogs we know, Bozo's well trained. And no-one minds him wandering in and out of yards. He's perfect!"

I could hear Jye's reluctance. "I don't know. Do you think it could work?"

"Let me put it this way—have you got a better plan?"

"I suppose not ..." he answered.

"You know, a little bit of enthusiasm wouldn't hurt here!" I told him.

"I'm sorry, Matt," he answered. "I guess we could try. I'll bring Bozo over in the morning."

I have to admit that by the time he arrived with Bozo, Jye was sounding more like his old self.

It didn't take us long to get Bozo fitted up. But this time, we had added a teeny microphone that let us give Bozo instructions. So now we could talk to Bozo as well as see and hear him!

"I wonder what Bozo does all day. He's never home," Jye said, as we watched him go.

It was still pretty early and Jye couldn't stay, but I told him that I'd keep an eye on the screen. It wasn't like I had anything else to do…

At first, it looked like being more fun than I had expected. Like when old Mr Bond sneaked out his front door in his pajamas and "borrowed" Mr Frith's newspaper. Then Mr Frith came out, looked for his paper, scratched his head and went back inside. About an hour later, Mr Bond snuck back out again and tossed the newspaper up onto Mr Frith's steps!

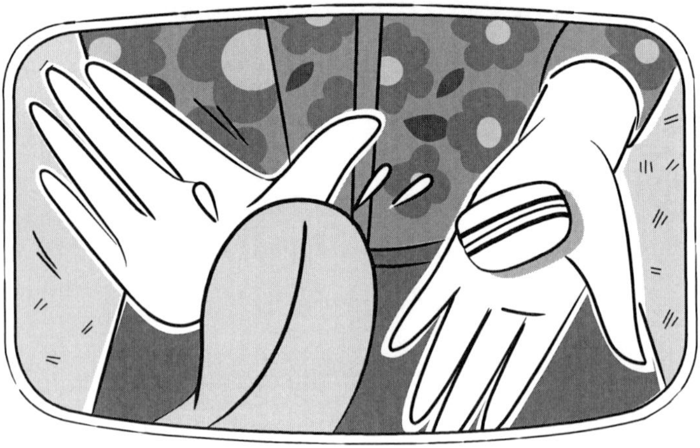

This was hilarious, because I'd heard Mr Frith complaining to my mum about how his paper is always late!

The more I watched, the more I realised that Bozo had it made! He went from one house to the next, and everyone gave him treats or cuddles.

Everyone talked to Bozo! Even people who didn't talk to other people!

By the way they spoke to him, it was pretty clear his visit to them was a daily routine.

This could be great!

It wasn't, though, and by evening I knew two things:

1. We lived in a boring neighbourhood.
2. Dogs were totally gross.

Chapter 7

Dogs Are Disgusting!

JYE WANDERED back in the next day, just when Bozo was being disgusting again. The screen showed part of a bush.

"What's that noise?" he said. "It sounds like water."

I shook my head. "What do you think it is? And it's about the seventy-fifth time today! That dog of yours has a problem!"

Jye started to laugh.

"Don't laugh! It was only funny the first time. Then it got worse. You should see the disgusting things your dog sticks his nose into! I'm just glad this camera hasn't got smell-o-phone!"

Jye was still chuckling, but I was getting bored.

"We live in the most boring street on Earth! Nothing happens!"

"Nothing at all?"

I sighed. "Well, the postie came. And we now know why Mr Frith's paper is always late." I shrugged my shoulders. "Apart from that—nothing."

Right then, my door burst open and Angie stormed in. And she was mad. "Okay, squirt, where is it?"

I frowned. "Where's what?"

"My portable DVD player. I can't find it anywhere, so that leaves you. Hand it over."

I was innocent, I really was! "I haven't seen it. Honest!"

She tapped her foot. "Don't play games, Matt. Just give it back."

I jumped up off the bed—for two reasons. Sure, I was mad I was being accused of something I hadn't done.

But also, the look on Jye's face reminded me that I had to make sure Angie didn't see the screen! She'd guess what we were doing. And then she'd guess I'd "borrowed" Sam's gear!

I moved away from the computer. "I truly haven't got it, Ange! I haven't seen it! I've been stuck in here all day!"

Jye moved so that he was blocking the computer screen. "Where did you last have it? My mum says to trace your steps backwards and you should find what you've lost ..."

Angie's shoulders slumped.

"I had it yesterday afternoon," she said. "I can't remember what I did with it. I was on the phone for a while and then I was looking at the new samples with Mum…"

She was walking out as she was talking, so for once she must have believed me.

That was a good thing, but the relief running through me was because she hadn't caught our web-cam.

Whew! That was close.

A noise on the screen made us both turn.

"It's just the delivery guys again," Jye muttered. "Boy! Everyone in this whole area must be getting free stuff!"

Bozo was obviously resting because we had a clear, still picture. The camera wasn't swinging around making me seasick this time. I could see right up to the guy's pockets as he carried the box.

Then Bozo turned back to the truck. The other guy was there, shifting boxes around.

Jye shrugged and we watched the first guy come back out. Bozo must have finished resting because he hopped up and trotted over to him, running around his legs and jumping up at him. I started to get dizzy again.

But it was pretty boring. I'd just started to turn away when I saw something…

Chapter 8

Good Doggie!

"DID YOU SEE something in that guy's pocket then?"

"Dunno. Just his grotty hankie, maybe," Jye answered.

I scratched my head. I was sure I'd seen something. I was watching carefully now. The guy was almost at the truck and Bozo had skipped along with him.

"Good boy, Boz," I muttered. "Stay with the guys."

"Why?" Jye asked.

"I don't know really. There was just something ..."

"You've been watching too much TV since you were grounded," Jye said, as he shook his head.

"Yeah, well, maybe all that TV has paid off. Listen!" I put my hand up to shush him. The delivery guys were talking.

"Not much in there," the first one was saying quietly. "Think we've got most of the good stuff already. Picked up one last trinket ..."

Then he pulled a gold chain from his pocket. It sparkled for a moment.

"Trinket! That's what I saw!" I whispered. I turned up the sound and focused on their voices.

"Stay, Bozo. Good dog, stay," Jye was whispering into the microphone.

"I think I've got the next one scoped, though," the first guy continued. "Kids leave lots of stuff lying around. Got a nice, sparkly sample yesterday. Good thing kitties can't talk, huh?" he finished on a chuckle.

We both gasped. "They're the thieves!" Jye yelled. "I've got to tell Mum!"

I pulled at his T-shirt as he tried to whiz past. "Wait! Think about this!"

He slowed and frowned. ""What?"

"We don't have any real proof. They didn't actually say they'd stolen anything," I said.

"Jye," I continued, "unless we can prove these guys did it, people around here will still think it was you!"

Jye slumped back onto my bed. "Well, what can I do?"

"We've got to catch them in the act!"

"How?" he asked.

I shrugged. "I suppose the first thing is to work out where they're going to hit next."

"They said they'd picked up a sparkly sample," Jye said, thinking out loud. "I suppose we have to try and find out who had some jewellery stolen yesterday."

"I agree," I told him, "but that's going to be really hard. You can't ask because half the street isn't talking to you! And I'm grounded ..."

"We could start with which houses have kids," he suggested. "That would narrow it down ..."

We were making lists when my door burst open again. Didn't anyone EVER knock around here?

"That's it! I'm not playing any more games! Hand the DVD player over, Matthew! I've searched everywhere! Joke's over. Give it back or you'll be in so much trou—"

Angie stopped mid-sentence and her eyes opened wide. "What's this?"

My heart sank. She was pointing straight at the computer screen.

"Are you spying on the street? How did you ...?"

Then her eyes got even wider. "You took Sam's equipment! You little sneak! Right!" she said as she turned. "SAM!"

I don't know how or why—but it suddenly hit me.

"Wait! Ange, wait! I know who has it." My heart was really thudding now. "What's worse—I know whose house is next on their hit list ..."

Chapter 9

Payback Time

ANGIE SPUN BACK. "I knew you had something to do with this! When I tell Mum, you're going to be grounded for life!"

I put up both hands. "Angie, I promise I didn't take it." I turned to Jye. "Those guys—when they said they picked up a sparkly sample—they weren't talking about jewellery."

"What are you babbling on about?" Angie demanded.

"Ange? Describe your DVD player to Jye."

"Why?" Then she shrugged. "It's silver and it's covered in fake jewels. I did it one night when I was bored. It looks really cute, though …"

She stopped and turned back to me. "Why am I telling him this?"

"Sparkly!!" Jye yelled. "Not jewellery!" His voice dropped. "But that means …"

"Yep, it means we're the next house to be robbed." My heart really was racing hard now. "Angie? We're about to get robbed by the same people who stole your DVD player. And we need your help."

She shook her head. "This is just some sort of cover-up for taking my stuff. Why should I help you?"

I smiled.

It was an evil smile.

“Okay. But don’t blame me if certain video footage turns up. Smoochy stuff… I think your friends would *looove* it.” I clutched both my hands under my chin and stared at the ceiling, fluttering my eyelashes. “Oh honey-kins—I *looove* you so much… kissy kissy kissy…”

Her mouth dropped open and she couldn’t say a word.

Trust me—that was a first for Angie!

“Are we even now?” I asked with a chuckle. “Now, let’s get Sam.”

Sam arrived, and I quickly explained. For the first time ever, they both listened to me. All Sam said was, “How did you get the stuff from my room?”

I was hoping to gloss over that part, but I figured it was time for the truth. I told him, then held my breath while he thought about what I’d said.

“The sprinkler? You lured me out there on purpose? You tricked me?”

Sam's eyes got bigger with every word. And his voice got higher.

And my face got redder. That happens when you hold your breath. And that's what I'd been doing. I'd known this wasn't going to be easy.

For a second, I hoped maybe I'd just pass out from lack of oxygen, but then I remembered Jye. And the thieves.

I nodded, waiting.

Suddenly Sam grinned. "Nice work, little bro'! You might turn out okay after all."

I let out my breath and gave a huge whoop. "So you'll help?"

Sam nodded. "I'm in. What did you have in mind?"

Chapter 10

Go, Hot Dog!

OUR BIGGEST PROBLEM was working out when the delivery men would strike.

Angie frowned. "The survey period ends this weekend. That means there's only today and tomorrow left."

"Have we had a delivery today?" I asked.

She shook her head. "I've been waiting."

"It won't matter," said Sam. "We'll get everything set up. I'll get cameras coming from four angles. As soon as they lift the goods, we'll call the police. They'll nab them before they get too far."

The next step was to set a really tempting trap. We put a box at the front door. On the top sat some things that looked really valuable—like Grandma's DVD player (broken!), my old electronic games, a wallet filled with folded newspaper, and some other stuff. Underneath this stuff were some old clothes and towels to make it look real.

The truth was, it was all pretty worthless. Well, we didn't want to lose any of our "good" stuff, just in case our plan failed!

"Right, we're set then. Now we just have to wait," Sam said. Then he frowned. "Matt? What are you doing?"

I looked up guiltily. "Oh, um, I was just adding a few more 'trinkets'—just to make it more tempting."

"Those are Mum's collectibles! They're expensive!" Angie hissed.

"Yeah—but they're ugly, too," I muttered. But I put them back anyway.

The next hour or so was probably the best time I'd had all holidays. All four of us sat around in the kitchen and talked. We even played cards. I couldn't remember having so much fun with my brother and sister before.

Suddenly, the doorbell rang.

"This could be it. Everybody ready?" Sam whispered. "It should be really smooth, so don't panic. Okay, Ange, go!"

Angie swallowed and ran to the door. We stayed and watched on Sam's laptop. I noticed Angie look back at the cameras before she opened up.

"Oh, hi!" she said. "Just bring them in. Sorry about the box—I'm packing to go away with my friends."

The man asked for a pen—just like he always did. That's how they scoped the place.

Angie took her time as we'd planned. While she was gone, the man looked around. Then he bent down and slipped the wallet into his pocket. In the next few minutes, he'd taken everything except Grandma's DVD player. Only because it was too big to fit into his pockets!

It was smooth. Unless you knew exactly what was there, you might not notice for hours that stuff was missing.

Then he moved and he was out of sight.

Oh, no! How did that happen!

I jumped up and started to creep along the hall before I even thought about what I was doing.

And almost walked right into the man's arms! There he was, rummaging through an old bag of Angie's that she'd left there.

I don't know who got the bigger fright, me or him!

My mouth started to open, but before I could say anything, he grabbed me.

"Listen here, you pipsqueak! You say one word and I'll make sure you pay! Right?"

Staying quiet wasn't something I was good at. So I *yelled*. Loud and long.

"Let my brother go!" Sam warned from behind me.

"No way!" yelled the man. "I'm not letting you kids stop me now!"

He started dragging me towards the door and then the most amazing thing happened. The guy was suddenly attacked from three sides!

Both Angie and Sam lunged, and Hot Dog was the third!

HOT DOG??

Angie and Sam both grabbed me. They didn't have to do anything else because Hot Dog had the guy by the trousers and the growls coming from him were enough to scare even me!

Wow! I guessed Hot Dog saved his courage (and energy) for special occasions. Thank goodness!

Jye sped around the corner with the phone. "The police are on their way."

After the police had taken away the delivery guys, I looked at my brother and sister. "Hey, thanks guys. That was pretty brave ..."

Angie ruffled my hair. "Well, you ARE our brother. And no-one messes with him—but us!" she said with a laugh.

I smiled. "And Sam? I'm sorry I took your stuff. But thanks for helping me. I didn't even have to blackmail you."

Sam grinned. "You know, squirt, I don't mind you using some of my stuff. I just mind that you never ask. Just ask in future!"

Then he frowned. "By the way, where's the camera gear you took?"

Bozo! "Oh, no!"

I dived upstairs and there was the doggie-cam still recording. And there was Bozo in Mr Bond's kitchen. He was drinking out of a glass on a low bench.

I squinted. There was something in the glass. "*Ewwww!* That's Mr Bond's false teeth!"

Sam laughed and rubbed his hands together. "Looks like I just won the next Funniest Home Video comp!"

"You!! It was my idea …"

"And my dog!"

"Ahh—but my equipment. Sorry, squirts. Now, if only you'd asked …" he said, giving an evil chuckle.